UPLIFT

CONQUER SELF-DOUBT, STRESS, AND OVERTHINKING TO LIVE YOUR BEST LIFE

SHARAD RAJ C

Contents

CHAPTER I

Low mood

"I have been depressed since the past few weeks, I don't know what has happened, or how it started, but all of a sudden I don't feel like doing anything, I feel like something is missing, I used to do a lot of things before but now they don't interest me. I have stopped doing everything, I feel lonely and I don't know how to deal with it."

When a potential client reaches out for therapy, I quickly provide the necessary information to start the sessions. While handling these details, I find myself wondering about the root cause of their distress—how long they've been feeling this way, any specific triggers, or recent life events that might have contributed.

My first priority, however, is to offer a supportive presence and genuinely listen. It's crucial to create an environment where the client feels truly seen and heard, setting the stage for us to explore their struggles together.

As I think this through, I'm reminded of behavioural activation—a therapeutic approach that could be helpful here. It involves encouraging clients to re-engage in activities they once enjoyed, helping to lift their mood and promote positive change.

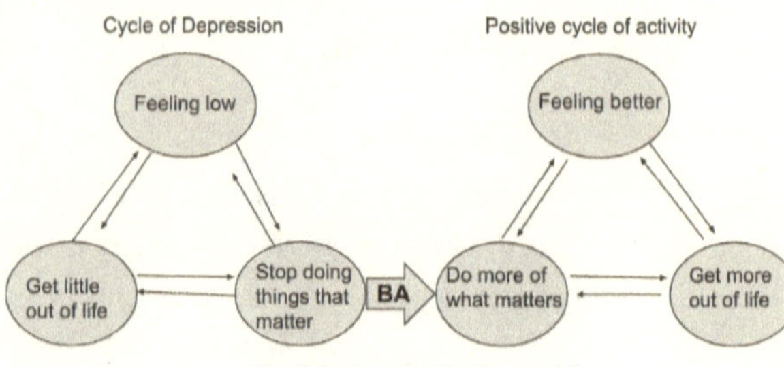

The Behavioural activation model

This approach helps in restructuring our mood, making us feel better. As easy as this approach seems, it is difficult to suddenly shift to doing all the things that you liked doing when you are not even doing the basic things.

It is certainly a slow progress that you make, and for that to happen there needs to be a certain set of activities that you should plan on doing. You can plan your activities from "Most easy" to "Most difficult". Example, right now, getting up from your bed and going on a walk might be the most difficult thing to do, but listening to some soothing music might be the most easy task to do. So, to begin with, prioritise listening to calm music, and gradually include tasks that seem difficult. Make sure you are covering your BASE.

Cover your **BASE**	Monday	Tuesday
Build Social life	Connect with an Old friend	Meet my best friend
Accomplish	Finish a pending task	Go for a morning walk
Self-care	Exercise for 30 minutes	Bath
Explore	Read a new book	Go to a new place

Activity scheduling through BASE

Meet a friend	Do Cleaning	Watch a movie	Travel to your favourite place
Start writing a journal	Call up an old friend	Practice Mindfulness	Set an achievable goal
Start a new hobby	Visit a friend	Do gardening	Exercise daily
Learn new things	Skin care	Meditate	Create a vision board

Activity list for BASE

You can actively work toward enhancing your emotional state by exercising self control and resisting the urges that are driven by your present state of mind. Rather than giving in to your emotions, you take charge of your behaviour and direct it in the direction of actions that support a more optimistic outlook. This resistance to your pessimistic thoughts acts as a trigger for improvement, gradually changing your mood's course to one of optimism. It's a subtle but effective kind of self-regulation in which every instance of resistance turns into a victory against the pull of negativity, eventually opening the door to a happier and more resilient state of mind.

My thoughts again shift to other interventions that could work for any one with a low mood, because different Interventions work for different people. And just then I get an email from the client.

"Unfortunately I don't have the money for therapy right now, I was hoping you could give me some advice, but anyway, thank you."

I stare at the email with a blank expression on my face. Although the professional in me knew that I wouldn't be able to be there for everyone, everytime, the therapist in me wanted to help the client.

CHAPTER II

Motivation

"I don't feel like doing the things that I used to do, and no matter how much I really want to try doing those things, It doesn't happen. I think of doing it, everyday, but I don't end up doing it and it goes on and on.."

Everyone at some point loses interest in doing the things that they used to do and no matter how much they try pushing themselves to do those things, they hardly are able to continue doing it for a longer time and then they eventually give up.

To be precise, you might have been fully motivated to start exercising in the beginning but might have slowly stopped. You might have thought to do something on your self development but might have slowly lost motivation to continue doing so.

Irrespective of how important that thing was, most of the people move on and they stop thinking about what they are supposed to do. They get busy, they handle other important commitments, or they simply keep themselves entertained and then it doesn't matter anymore. The time they had given on seriously thinking about what they should start doing in their lives goes in vain. Even though all of this keeps going on in the background we all feel like we are doing everything and are happy until a low moment hits again.

Once a low moment hits, we are again in the stage of awakening. We get back to thinking of all the important things we should start doing, like exercising or self development or doing a little reading.. Suddenly a little guilt creeps in for not being able to do the same things before. But then we assure ourselves that it's not going to be the same this time and we will show some self discipline. The result of this most often is, it all goes good in the beginning but eventually we lose the motivation and the same cycle continues again. Honestly, this happens with most of us and there might be different reasons for it.

Breaking the no motivation cycle:

In this journey of trying to keep yourself motivated to do certain things, the first thing that becomes important is Identifying. Try to **identify** what it is that you want to achieve, and how much work and effort would it actually take for you to achieve it. When Identifying try to not write down too many things and be very specific with what you want to achieve.

Then try to put down a **timeline** you think that would be needed to achieve what you planned. If the timeline is too long, try to break down your timeline in a shorter period and indicate how much of what you are planning to achieve will be completed in that short timeline.

Make sure that the goal that you plan on achieving aligns with your **purpose.** Because the more important that the goal is to you, the more motivated you will be to achieve that goal. During this process make sure that you are **reviewing** your progress every week by writing down what went right and what was challenging for you during the week in doing what you had planned and finally time by time, make **plans** to overcome your challenges.

The process	Date - dd/mm/yyyy
Identify What is something that you really want to do/achieve?	I want to lose 2 kilograms of weight so I want to start exercising.
Set a timeline How much time would you require to achieve this goal?	I might require a month to lose 2 kilograms. I will lose 1 kilogram in the next 15 days.
Purpose What is the need for achieving this goal?	By achieving this goal I will feel more confident about the way I look, and I would feel a lot more positive for achieving what I plan.
Review (After a week) What is working out well and what are some challenges you are facing to achieve this goal?	I was very motivated for the beginning two days and I spent a lot of time exercising. But I have been facing difficulties with lack of consistency. I skipped exercising the last two days.
Plan What are some of the ways to tackle the challenges you are facing?	I will try to have an exercise buddy. We will both set challenges and see who achieves the challenge for that particular day. I think that would push me to be consistent.

Breaking the no motivation cycle

Making a plan gets challenging, because we are generally not able to follow the plans that we usually make, or we are simply unsure of what to plan. The secret to making a good plan and following it is to not be too ambitious. Before we make a plan the question that should be asked is, *was I able to Implement a similar plan like this before?* While making a plan it is important to consider what is going right, and if the plan made is really achievable. As you start implementing your plans and make progress towards what you want to achieve and you are seeing the results of it, you automatically feel motivated to perform the action again. That is how the no motivation cycle is finally broken.

Motivational drive:

The motivational drive within us helps us to perform any work or task. Once that drive is full, we are able to make the best use of our potential, and achieve the goals set. But once we have no drive, we fail at doing tasks, or we keep procrastinating the tasks we have at hand. Hence having a motivational drive becomes important to complete a task and for the drive to last long it is Important to have Internal motivation rather than external.

Motivation	Meaning	Goals
Intrinsic (Internal)	You do the work because it is fulfilling on an internal level. Perhaps you engage in it because it's satisfying, fulfilling, and fun.	Your basic psychological needs for autonomy, competence, and relatedness are satisfied when you achieve your goals, which originate from within.
Extrinsic (External)	You do the work in order to get an external reward in return.	These Goals don't satisfy your basic psychological needs. They are only focused on external gains, such as money, fame, power, or avoiding consequences.

Types of Motivation

We might really like it when someone praises us for the work that we do, and that might motivate us to work more efficiently. We might be told that we will be promoted if we do a set number of tasks for that year and we might instantly be motivated to complete the set tasks in the given year. But what if we don't get promoted even after that? Where would all the motivation go? This sort of a motivation is always dependent on others and other external factors therefore there are high chances of it not lasting long.

But irrespective of getting promoted or not, what if we looked at completing the set tasks as an opportunity for us to gain experience and understand the nature of work? We would still be motivated to do the work even if we are not promoted. The reason the motivational drive lasts longer with this kind of approach is because we are internally driven rather than just focusing on achieving external gains. Hence, the secret to staying motivated is to make sure that the Motivational drive is always full.

However, I don't think this one technique will make you more motivated overnight; instead, you have to start by making small changes and then make a few more changes until you figure out what works best for you.

CHAPTER III

Stress

During my Interaction with different students the most common thing they say *is i feel stressed*. And even though the word itself seems stressful, stress is nothing but pressure or tension that is caused when a lot of things are going on in our lives at the same time. It's a common thing - we all at some point in our lives might have had a lot that came up which might have caused extreme worry and we found it difficult to deal with.

Earlier, because people had good social support, and because things were not as fast paced as now, most of them were able to deal with their worries effectively. But things have drastically changed now.

We all have become more competitive, we expect a lot from our lives and we want to keep earning more money to fulfil the needs of ourselves and our family. There has been a shift in the dynamics, children are expected to read a lot to be successful and adults are expected to work a lot to provide for their family. There has been a lack of healthy balance between work and personal lives. When all of this is already going on and an uncertainty knocks the door, there are high chances of it causing extreme worry or stress.

The good part is there has been vast knowledge everywhere on ways to manage stress, and most of them are aware of what stress is.. But what is lacking is wisdom. You tell someone that you are going through stress and the first thing that they will probably say is, do meditation.

Most of them are unaware of how something will help, but they just blindly follow the quick fix tips that come in handy. Meditation definitely helps to calm down and de-intensify your emotions and thoughts, but what if you are going through a stressful situation every single day, and it's only intensifying your thoughts and emotions, even meditation might not help.

Whenever a stressful situation arises, the way we think of the situation plays a crucial role in defining our emotions, and this in turn will influence the behaviours that we perform.

Let's say you recently got to know that you are about to lose your job in a month, and you don't have any savings or you were not prepared for this moment, you suddenly start thinking that you have not upskilled enough and you might find it hard to get another job, you have expenses to meet and you start think of how you wouldn't have money after a month and then the spiral of thoughts don't stop. One after the other the thoughts keep coming and you feel nothing but worse, you are not happy anymore and you don't have interest in doing any activities, this makes you feel even more worse and it only intensifies your negative thoughts.

What if you had a similar situation but instead of thinking that you would not find a job in the next month, you started to think of how many jobs you could probably apply to and how much amount of time you still have left, and that you can actually upskill a little everyday for this whole one month, giving interviews whenever necessary. This whole thought would shift your mood to a more positive one and in turn you would be more inspired to do the work that is required to get a new job.

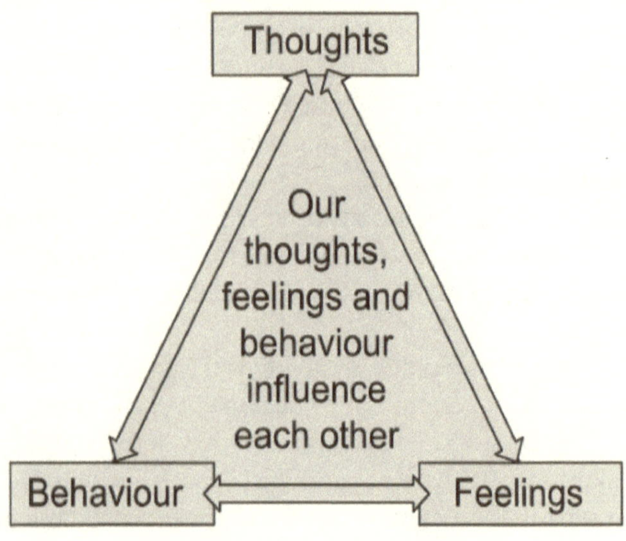

The Cognitive triangle

It might not be as easy as said, because if restructuring our thoughts was that easy we wouldn't have so many mental health professionals available to support the emotional needs of people.

The way we think is influenced by the core beliefs that we have about ourselves, and this core belief is the part of our personality formed right in our childhood. So it is definitely difficult to reframe our thoughts if the core belief that we have is the opposite to what we are trying to think. If you are trying to think that everything is going to be okay, but your core belief says that things have never been okay, it is impossible to suddenly shift your thoughts to a positive one. So it takes a lot of work, and constant determination to rewire our thoughts to ones that are helpful to us, hence maintaining a thought record might help.

Date	What happened?	Thoughts?	Emotion and Intensity?	Reframed thought
dd/mm/yyyy	Example: I am about to lose my job.	I am such a loser, I don't plan anything, I'll never be good enough	Guilt: 8/10 Anxious: 7/10	I might not have planned everything but it doesn't make me a loser because if I was a loser I wouldn't have reached till here. I'll try to learn from this and do better next time
What core beliefs are coming up?		How can you reframe the beliefs?		
"I am not good enough"		I know I might be imperfect, but I also know that I can do certain things very well. I am constantly trying to improve and I know that I'll be a better version of myself eventually. At the same time I accept myself and love myself for whoever I am today.		

Thought record and challenging core beliefs

One of the first steps to getting rid of negative thoughts is to keep a thought journal so you can examine and address your thoughts. Rewiring your negative thoughts will undoubtedly take some time, but the effort will be worthwhile.

Once your unhelpful thoughts are rewired to helpful thoughts, the general way of looking at a stressful situation also changes, reducing the intensity of your emotion and the way you react. Therefore the key to reducing your worry in a stressful situation lies in working on your thoughts. It can always be the other way around as well, for some exercising and meditation might help, as it directly influences the way we feel, which in turn will have an impact on our behaviour and thoughts.

However, It is most effective to use a three-pronged strategy, where you work on rewiring your negative beliefs, engage in behaviours that incline you toward your goals, and take actions that impact your emotions.

CHAPTER IV

Anxiety

Anxiety often feels like an invisible weight pressing down on you—a constant hum of worry and unease that clouds your thoughts and steals your peace. It's not just in your mind; it shows up in your body too, with racing heartbeats, tense muscles, or sleepless nights. At its worst, anxiety can make even simple tasks feel overwhelming, leaving you stuck in a cycle of fear and avoidance.

But here's the thing about anxiety: it's not a permanent state. It's a response—a reaction to uncertainty, pressure, or perceived threats. While you may not have control over when it shows up, you do have the power to influence how it affects you. The key is to focus on small, meaningful steps that guide you toward calm and confidence.

Turning your focus toward the future:
When anxiety dominates your thoughts, it's easy to get stuck in the present challenges or past regrets. But what if, instead of focusing on what feels wrong, you shifted your attention to what could be?

Imagine a version of yourself who feels calm and capable, free from the weight of anxiety. What would your day look like? How would you spend your time? How would you approach challenges differently?

This isn't about escaping the present—it's about giving yourself a clear picture of where you want to go. When you have a vision for the future, you create a sense of direction, even in moments of uncertainty. Visualising a better version of yourself opens the door to possibility and helps you see that change is not only achievable but within your reach.

Identifying what's already working:
Anxiety often has a way of magnifying what feels wrong and making you overlook what's right. Yet, no matter how overwhelming life may seem, there are always aspects where you're already succeeding. Recognizing these areas is the first step toward building a path forward.

Take a moment to reflect on situations where you've managed anxiety, even if just for a moment. What helped you feel calmer? Was it a particular activity, a mindset, or a small decision? These moments hold valuable insights about what works for you.

By focusing on what's already working, you shift your perspective. You're no longer trying to "fix" yourself; instead, you're building on the strengths and strategies you already have.

Setting clear, meaningful goals:
Anxiety thrives in uncertainty, so creating a clear sense of direction can be incredibly grounding. Instead of focusing on eliminating anxiety altogether, consider what you'd like to achieve despite it.
Ask yourself:

- *What's the first small change I'd like to see in my life?*
- *How will I know I'm making progress?*
- *What would success look like, even in the smallest way?*

The key is to focus on achievable, meaningful goals that give you a sense of purpose. These don't have to be monumental. Sometimes, the simplest goals—like getting through a morning routine calmly or taking a deep breath before a challenging conversation—can set the stage for larger changes.

Breaking the cycle:

Anxiety often feels like a loop, with the same thoughts and worries repeating endlessly. Breaking that cycle starts with small, intentional actions.

Consider how you might approach a single moment of anxiety differently. Could you pause and take a deep breath? Could you shift your focus to what's within your control? Could you ask yourself what one small action you could take to move forward?

Each step you take, no matter how small, interrupts the cycle. Over time, these small actions build momentum, replacing patterns of fear with patterns of progress.

Building on strengths:

Everyone has unique strengths that can help them navigate challenges, even when anxiety feels overwhelming. These strengths might include problem-solving skills, creativity, resilience, or the ability to connect with others.

Take a moment to identify your strengths. How have they helped you in the past? How might you use them now to move forward?

By focusing on what you're good at, you remind yourself that you're not defined by your anxiety. Your strengths are always there, ready to support you as you create the life you want.

Celebrating progress:

Progress isn't always about dramatic changes. It's about recognizing and celebrating the small steps you take every day. When you acknowledge your efforts, you reinforce the belief that change is possible and build confidence in your ability to move forward.

Even if the progress feels small—getting out of bed on a tough day, making a decision you've been avoiding, or taking a few deep breaths during a moment of stress—it's worth celebrating. These moments remind you that you're capable of overcoming challenges and creating a brighter future.

Creating a ripple effect:
One of the most empowering aspects of overcoming anxiety is that every small step you take creates a ripple effect. When you take control of one aspect of your life, it often spills over into others, making change feel more natural and sustainable.

For example, a single act of self-care, like going for a walk or setting aside time to relax, can lead to greater energy and focus. That energy might help you tackle a project or engage more fully with loved ones. Over time, these ripples build into lasting change, helping you create a life that feels calmer and more fulfilling.

Moving forward with confidence
Anxiety doesn't define you, and it doesn't have to control your life. By shifting your focus to what's possible, identifying your strengths, and taking small, intentional steps, you can move beyond its grip towards a life of calm and confidence.

Change doesn't happen all at once. It's the small, consistent actions that make the biggest difference. With each step you take, you're not just managing anxiety—you're reclaiming your peace of mind and building a future you're excited to embrace.

Remember, you're not alone on this journey. The path to overcoming anxiety is within you, and every effort you make brings you closer to the calm and confident version of yourself that's waiting to emerge.

CHAPTER V

Overthinking

Overthinking is like being caught in a maze, except that here there's no exit. You replay situations over and over, imagine the worst possible outcomes, or question every choice you've made or need to make. It feels endless and exhausting, draining your energy without offering any real answers. Instead of leading to solutions, overthinking creates more stress and leaves you feeling stuck.

We've all been there. Maybe you've spent sleepless nights reliving a conversation, asking yourself, *"Did I say the wrong thing?"* Or perhaps you've hesitated to make a decision because you were too busy analysing every possible *"what-if."* Overthinking tricks you into believing that thinking harder or longer will help you avoid mistakes or find the perfect answer.

But here's the truth: overthinking isn't a sign of being extra careful or thorough. It's a habit—a mental trap that keeps you spinning in circles. The more you overanalyze, the harder it becomes to act. Instead of protecting you, it often leaves you feeling overwhelmed and paralyzed. The good news is that you don't have to stay stuck. Overthinking is something you can learn to manage and eventually overcome.

The cycle of overthinking:
Let's start by understanding how overthinking works. Picture this: You've received a text from a friend that seems unusually short. Immediately, your mind jumps into action:

- *"Did I do something wrong?"*

- *"Maybe they're upset with me."*
- *"Should I apologise for something?"*

Instead of texting back to clarify, you spend hours analysing every recent interaction, replaying past conversations, and imagining all the ways they might feel offended. The more you think, the worse you feel. Sounds familiar?

This is the cycle of overthinking: a triggering event leads to worry, which then fuels unhelpful thoughts, creating a spiral of anxiety or indecision. Breaking the cycle requires stepping back and changing how you respond.

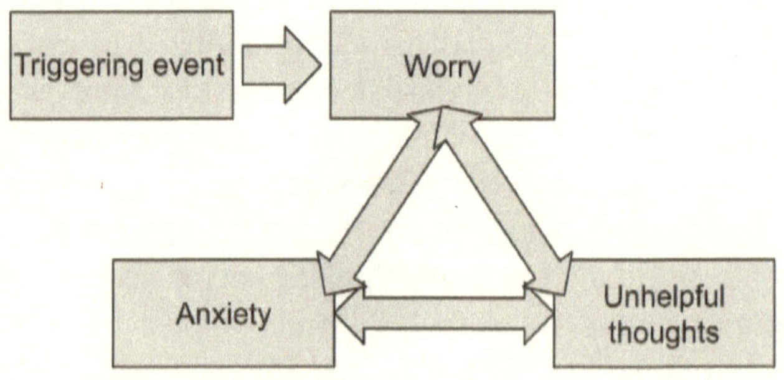

Breaking the Cycle with Perspective:
One of the most powerful tools against overthinking is perspective. When caught in a mental loop, your thoughts can feel like absolute truths. But they're often just assumptions, distorted by fear or uncertainty.
Consider Raj, an IT professional who couldn't stop replaying a conversation with his manager. He was worried that he had come across as unprepared during their meeting. For days, Raj overthought about every word he

had said, convinced his manager thought less of him. But when he finally gathered the courage to ask for feedback, his manager praised his enthusiasm and engagement.

Overthinking blinds us to reality. By challenging our assumptions and seeking evidence, we can often find that our fears are unfounded. A simple shift in perspective can break the cycle and bring relief.

Exercise: Reframe the Thought

Write down one overthinking thought you're having. Then, rewrite it with a balanced perspective.

- Overthinking Thought: *"I'm going to fail this presentation."*
- Balanced Perspective: *"I've prepared for this. It's normal to feel nervous, but I can handle it."*

Focus on what you can control:
Overthinking often revolves around things you can't change: the past, other people's opinions, or hypothetical outcomes. Shifting your focus to what's within your control can help you regain a sense of power and direction.

For example, if you're overthinking an upcoming exam, ask yourself:

- *What actions can I take right now to prepare?*
- *How can I make the best use of my time today?*

Rather than spiralling into *"What if I don't pass?"* focus on studying one topic at a time. Action breaks the cycle of overthinking by shifting your energy toward solutions instead of problems.

> **Exercise: Create an Action Plan**
>
> 1. Identify the issue you're overthinking about.
> 2. Write down three small steps you can take to address it.
> 3. Commit to completing one step today.

Set boundaries with your thoughts:
Overthinking often takes up more time and energy than it deserves. Setting boundaries with your thoughts helps you take control of when and how much you think about an issue.

One technique is to schedule "worry time." For example, if you're overthinking a decision, set aside 15 minutes in the evening to focus on it. During that time, write down your concerns and explore possible solutions. When the time is up, close your notebook and move on.

Another boundary-setting technique is to redirect your attention when overthinking strikes. If you find yourself spiralling, engage in an activity that anchors you in the present—take a walk, listen to music, or practise deep breathing.

Embrace Imperfection:
Overthinking often stems from a fear of making mistakes or being less than perfect. But perfection is an impossible standard that fuels doubt and indecision.

Consider this: Have you ever spent hours overthinking an email, trying to phrase it perfectly, only to realise later that it didn't matter as much as you thought? Learning to embrace imperfection frees you to take action without the burden of unrealistic expectations.

> **Mantra:** Repeat to yourself: *"It's okay to do my best and let go of the rest."*

Take action, no matter how small:

Overthinking thrives on inaction. The longer you stay stuck in your thoughts, the harder it feels to move forward. Taking even the smallest step can disrupt the cycle and build momentum.

For example, if you're overthinking about starting a fitness routine, don't wait until you've researched the perfect workout plan. Start with a 10-minute walk today. Action doesn't have to be perfect—it just has to be intentional.

> **Exercise: The 5-Minute Rule**
>
> Commit to spending just 5 minutes on a task you've been overthinking. Often, starting is the hardest part, and once you begin, it's easier to keep going.

Practice self-compassion:

Overthinking often comes with self-criticism: *"Why can't I stop thinking about this?"* or *"What's wrong with me?"* This only makes the cycle worse. Instead, practise kindness toward yourself.

Treat yourself as you would treat a friend who's struggling. Remind yourself that overthinking is a common experience and doesn't define your worth or capability.

> **Start with an affirmation:**
> Write down one kind thing you can say to yourself when you catch yourself overthinking.
> *(Example: "I'm doing the best I can, and that's enough.")*

Overthinking is just a habit, and like any habit, you can unlearn it with time and practice. When you notice yourself spiralling, pause and ask, "Is this helping me?" If not, take a deep breath, focus on what's important, and take one small step forward. By questioning your thoughts, changing your perspective, taking small steps, letting go of perfection, and focusing on the present, you can break free.

You are not your thoughts, and you are not defined by your doubts. You are the actions you take, the progress you make, and the strength you show when you choose to move forward. So take that step, however small it may seem, and keep moving forward.

CHAPTER VI

Self doubt

Self-doubt is like an uninvited guest that shows up just when you're about to do something meaningful. It sneaks in when you're preparing for an important interview, whispering, *"What if you freeze up? What if they think you're not qualified?"* It lingers when you're about to start a new project, planting seeds of doubt like, *"What if you don't have what it takes to see this through?"* Or it rears its head when you're ready to share your ideas in a meeting, making you second-guess, *"What if my thoughts sound silly?"*

Self-doubt convinces you that you're not good enough, smart enough, or worthy enough to succeed. It can feel paralysing, casting a shadow over your goals and dreams. Yet, self-doubt is not a complete enemy. The true challenge lies in how we respond to it.

Overcoming self-doubt isn't about silencing the critical voice within us but about changing how we see and respond to it. It means accepting its presence without letting it control our actions or limit our potential. By learning to live with self-doubt and viewing it as a natural part of growth, we can use it to reflect, build resilience, and move forward with purpose, instead of letting it hold us back.

Living with self-doubt:
The first step in overcoming self-doubt is acknowledging its presence. Pretending it doesn't exist or trying to push it away often gives it more power. When you accept self-doubt as a natural part of growth, you remove its ability to derail you.

Imagine this: you're standing at the edge of a diving board, ready to jump into the pool. Self-doubt might whisper, *"What if you fall awkwardly? What if you don't make a splash like everyone else?"* Instead of arguing with those thoughts, acknowledge them. Say to yourself, *"I hear you, and it's okay to feel this way."*

This approach creates space for self-doubt without letting it control your decisions. Acceptance doesn't mean agreeing with the doubts; it means recognizing their presence without judgement.

> **Practice:**
> The next time self-doubt arises, pause and name it. Say out loud or internally, *"This is self-doubt talking."* By identifying it, you distance yourself from its grip.

Separate yourself from the doubts:
Self-doubt thrives when you believe every thought it throws at you. But thoughts are just that—thoughts. They are not facts, nor do they define you.

When a thought like *"I'm not good enough"* appears, imagine it as a passing cloud in the sky. You are not the cloud; you are the observer, watching it drift by. This perspective helps you see self-doubt as temporary and separate from your true self.

> **Here's an exercise to try:**
>
> - Write down your self-doubting thoughts on paper.
> - Read them out loud, but add the phrase, *"I'm having the thought that..."* before each one. For example, instead of saying, *"I can't do this,"* say, *"I'm having the thought that I can't do this."*

This small shift reminds you that thoughts are fleeting. They don't have to dictate your actions or define your potential.

Ground yourself in the present:
Self-doubt often arises from fears of the future or regrets about the past. You might worry about failing, making mistakes, or not meeting expectations. These thoughts pull you away from the present moment, where your power lies.

Grounding yourself in the present can help quiet the noise of self-doubt. When your mind starts racing with self-critical thoughts, pause and focus on what's happening around you.

> **Exercise:**
>
> - Sit in a quiet space and take a few deep breaths.
> - Notice five things you can see, four things you can touch, three things you can hear, two things you can smell, and one thing you can taste.
> - Bring your attention back to the task at hand, focusing on what you can do right now to move forward.

By anchoring yourself in the present, you regain clarity and reduce the power of self-doubt to distract you.

Connect with what truly matters:
Self-doubt becomes louder when you lose sight of what's important to you. Reconnecting with your values—the things that give your life meaning—can help you move forward even when doubts linger.

Ask yourself:

- *What do I care about most in this situation?*
- *Why is this goal meaningful to me?*
- *Who do I want to be in the face of this challenge?*

For instance, if you're doubting your ability to speak up in a meeting, focus on the value behind your action. Perhaps it's your commitment to contributing to the team or sharing ideas that could make a difference. Let that value guide you, rather than the fear of self-doubt.

When you act in alignment with your values, you shift your focus from fear to purpose, allowing you to take meaningful steps even when doubts are present.

Take purposeful action:
Self-doubt often tricks you into waiting—waiting until you feel ready, confident, or certain. But waiting rarely leads to progress. The truth is, confidence often follows action, not the other way around.

Start small. Break your goal into manageable steps, and take the first one, no matter how small it seems. Each step forward builds momentum and weakens the grip of self-doubt.

Example:
If you're doubting your ability to write a book, start by

writing for ten minutes a day. Focus on completing a single page, rather than worrying about the entire project. Celebrate that step as progress.

Every action, no matter how small, is a victory over self-doubt. Over time, these small steps compound into significant growth.

Be kind to yourself:

Finally, remember that self-doubt is a shared human experience. Even the most successful people have faced moments of uncertainty. The difference lies in how they responded—with perseverance and self-compassion.

Treat yourself with the same kindness you'd offer a close friend. When you stumble, remind yourself that failure is part of growth. When doubts arise, counter them with gentle encouragement: *"It's okay to feel this way. I'm learning and growing with every step."*

> **Reflection:**
> Take a moment to acknowledge how far you've come, even with self-doubt as your companion. Celebrate your courage to keep moving forward.

The goal isn't to eliminate self-doubt—it's to change how you relate to it. Let it be a reminder that you're stepping outside your comfort zone, reaching for something that matters. Each time you take a step forward despite your doubts, you prove to yourself that you are capable, worthy, and strong.

You are more than your self-doubts. You are the actions you take, the values you uphold, and the progress you make. So take the leap, and watch as you rise.

Action Steps:

- **Write down one small step you'll take today to move forward:**
  (Example: "I will write the first draft of my presentation.")

  ____

- **What might self-doubt say when you take this step?**
  (Example: "This isn't good enough; you need more time.")

  ____

- **How will you respond to self-doubt in that moment?**
  (Example: "It's okay to feel this way. I'm making progress, and that's what matters.")

  ____

CHAPTER VII

Dealing with people

Within each of us is a unique blend of values, beliefs, ideas, and perspectives shaped by our experiences. Together, these create our internal response system, which guides how we interpret situations, interact with others, and handle challenges. This system acts like an inner compass, influencing our thoughts, feelings, and choices. Much of what we do - whether consciously or instinctively - comes from this response system. It affects how we react under stress, communicate, and navigate complex situations. As we grow and learn, this system evolves, shaping our daily actions and the impact we have on the world around us.

Formation of the Response system:
Our response system is shaped by several interconnected elements within an individual: core influences, internal filters, emotional responses, cognitive processing, behavioural responses, and a feedback loop. These elements work together, creating a unique internal framework that guides our reactions to the world around us. Each component influences the others, forming a continuous cycle where thoughts, feelings, and actions reinforce or adjust one another.

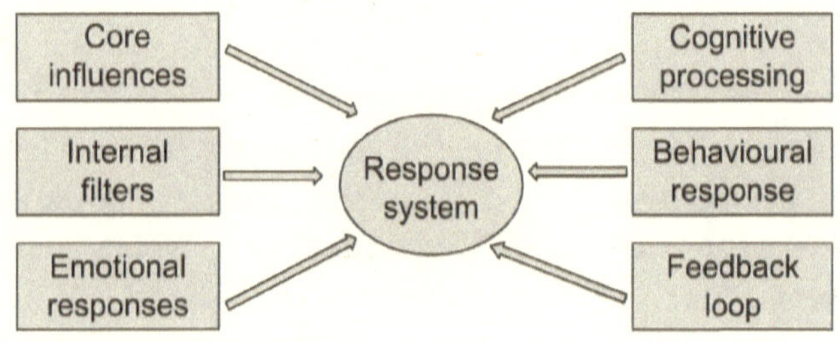

Formation of our response system

Core Influences include deeply rooted values, beliefs, personality traits, and past experiences that shape how we view the world and what we hold important. These are the foundational components that give direction to our reactions and decisions.

Internal Filters refer to the mental lenses through which we interpret situations. These filters, shaped by our expectations, attitudes, and biases, influence how we perceive people, events, and challenges, often shaping our reality before we consciously process it.

Emotional Responses are the feelings that arise as immediate reactions to our perceptions and experiences. Emotions like joy, anger, fear, or sadness serve as powerful drivers that can either motivate us or hinder our ability to respond effectively.

Cognitive Processing involves the thoughts and interpretations we form around an event or situation. This includes automatic thoughts, beliefs, and assumptions that influence how we make sense of what's happening and how we think we should respond.

Behavioral Response is the outward action or reaction we take in response to an event, based on the interaction of our emotions and thoughts. These actions can range from instinctual reactions to carefully considered responses.

The Feedback Loop occurs when the outcomes of our behaviour reinforce or reshape our core influences, beliefs, and future responses. Positive or negative results from our actions inform future behaviour, allowing us to adapt, refine, or change our response system over time.

How the Response system works:
Imagine you're facing a job interview; right away, several processes kick in, often without you noticing. First, your *core influences* come into play—your values, beliefs, and past experiences shape how you view the situation. If career success is important to you, you may feel extra urgency. If you've had tough interviews before, you might feel a mix of excitement and anxiety.

Next, your *internal filters* shape your expectations and assumptions. For instance, if you think the interviewer will be critical, you may feel more guarded even before stepping in the room. These filters set the tone for how you'll respond.

As the interview approaches, *emotional responses* surface—like anxiety, excitement, or self-doubt—which may even cause your heart to race. This is a natural reaction, happening almost instinctively.

At the same time, *cognitive processing* starts. Automatic thoughts like, "Will they like me?" or "What if I mess up?" emerges, affecting your confidence, depending on whether the thoughts are positive or negative. Your mind is working to make sense of the situation, shaping how you feel and act.

Then, *behavioural responses* kick in, guiding your actions. You might adjust your posture, take deep breaths to stay calm, or rehearse your answers in your mind—all without fully realising it. This is your response system preparing you to handle the interview.

Finally, a *feedback loop* comes into play throughout the interview. Each question, each reaction from the interviewer, and each moment provides feedback, shaping how you respond. If you get a positive reaction, your confidence may grow; if you stumble, self-doubt might increase. This ongoing feedback subtly adjusts your thoughts, emotions, and actions as the interview progresses.

Understanding people through response system:
Think about the last conversation you had with someone that really hurt you. Maybe you felt this way because you expected a more positive or understanding response but didn't get it. Often, we want others to truly understand us, especially those we've known for a long time. So, when their reaction falls short, it can be painful. We might even question, *"Do they really know me after all these years?"*

However, their response wasn't just about what you said or how well they know you. It had a lot to do with their own unique response system—the way their mind interprets and reacts to information. They may also have had certain expectations and assumptions, often unspoken, that influence how they respond. Their response system might tell them to stay neutral or avoid discussing emotions in tense situations. Or, they might interpret your feelings through their own experiences, thinking, "I'd handle this differently," without realising your needs and feelings may be different from theirs.

Understanding that people's reactions come from their own internal system can help us take things less personally. Rather than seeing their response as a reflection of how they feel about us, we can view it as part of their mental and emotional habits. This perspective can ease our own disappointment or hurt, making it easier to be compassionate.

The key to receiving a better response from others is clear communication. Each time you interact, their internal feedback loop is making mental notes about how you react. If you let things slide or don't express how you truly feel, they may assume their current way of responding is fine. Over time, this feedback loop reinforces their behaviour, so they continue responding the same way.

To change this, you need to communicate your needs openly and assertively, while maintaining a balanced approach. If something isn't okay, calmly let them know. By consistently expressing what you expect and what works for you, you help guide their feedback loop to adapt and respond more positively in future interactions.

The power of balance: Empathy and assertiveness

When dealing with people, the ability to balance our Interactions with both empathy and assertiveness can work wonders. Empathy is the ability to understand and connect with others' feelings, involving active listening and genuine interest. Assertiveness, on the other hand, is the skill of expressing our own thoughts, feelings, and needs openly and respectfully, standing up for ourselves while also respecting others.

Respond, don't react:

When responding to someone in a conflict or critical situation, take a moment to pause and reflect before reacting. This gives you the chance to understand the other person's response system—how their past experiences, values, and emotions influence their reaction. By doing this, you gain insight into why they might be saying what they're saying, which helps you avoid reacting too quickly or making assumptions. Listening actively and paying attention to their needs and feelings allows you to connect with them on a deeper level.

After considering the other person's perspective, it's important to reflect on your own feelings and needs. How is the situation affecting you? What do you need to feel respected or understood? Reflecting on your own emotional response helps you identify your boundaries and what's at stake for you, allowing you to approach the situation more calmly and respond in a balanced, constructive way.

The three-stage process:

Imagine two coworkers arguing about how to divide project responsibilities. One feels overwhelmed, and you're the other person. How would you respond? The three-stage process would help.

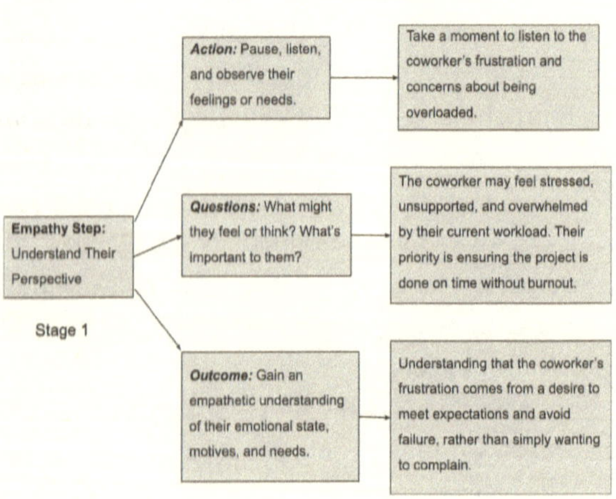

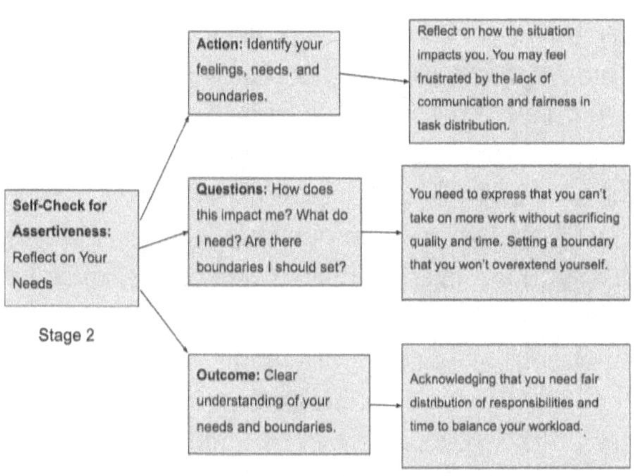

Action: Identify your feelings, needs, and boundaries.
Reflect on how the situation impacts you. You may feel frustrated by the lack of communication and fairness in task distribution.
Self-Check for Assertiveness: Reflect on Your Needs
Stage 2
Questions: How does this impact me? What do I need? Are there boundaries I should set?
You need to express that you can't take on more work without sacrificing quality and time. Setting a boundary that you won't overextend yourself.
Outcome: Clear understanding of your needs and boundaries.
Acknowledging that you need fair distribution of responsibilities and time to balance your workload.

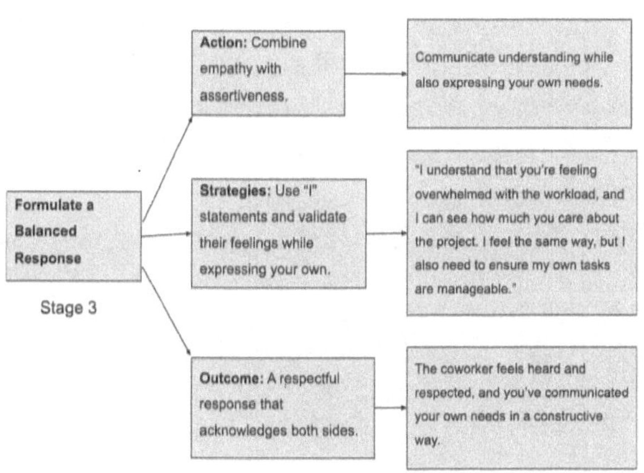

Action: Combine empathy with assertiveness.
Communicate understanding while also expressing your own needs.
Formulate a Balanced Response
Stage 3
Strategies: Use "I" statements and validate their feelings while expressing your own.
"I understand that you're feeling overwhelmed with the workload, and I can see how much you care about the project. I feel the same way, but I also need to ensure my own tasks are manageable."
Outcome: A respectful response that acknowledges both sides.
The coworker feels heard and respected, and you've communicated your own needs in a constructive way.

Developing the power of balance:

Many people understand the importance of maintaining a balanced approach of empathy and assertiveness in their interactions, yet they often struggle to put this into practice. For many, their response system—the habits and emotional patterns they've developed over time—creates challenges in communicating effectively.

Some feel too shy or lack confidence to speak up, while others struggle with emotions that quickly flare up in certain situations, making it hard to stay calm and assertive. These response patterns are deeply rooted, so they may end up either holding back or coming across too strongly, unable to find the ideal middle ground.

To develop this balance, we need to gradually rewire our response systems through practice. This means becoming more aware of our emotions, learning to manage them in the moment, and building communication skills that let us express our needs with both kindness and clarity. Over time, with consistent self reflection, we can boost our confidence, control our emotions, and connect with others in a way where conversations are filled with mutual respect.

Action points	Your response
Identify the Situation Describe a recent situation where you felt misunderstood, frustrated, or uncomfortable with someone.	
Recognize Your Initial Reaction How did you react in the moment? (Example: Did you feel angry, defensive, shy, or upset?)	
Understand Your Response System What beliefs or past experiences might have influenced your reaction? (Example: "I felt defensive because I've experienced criticism before in similar situations.")	
Evaluate Your Communication Style Did you communicate your needs clearly? (Example: "Did I speak up calmly, or did I hold back/overreact?")	
Set Intentions for Next Time How would you like to handle a similar situation in the future? (Example: "Next time, I want to stay calm and express my feelings clearly.")	
Practice Empathy Consider the other person's perspective. What might their response system look like? (Example: "They might have been acting out of stress or their own insecurities.")	
Commit to One Improvement Choose one specific way you can improve your response next time. (Example: "Take a deep breath before reacting.")	

Self reflection sheet

CHAPTER VIII

Moving on

When we go through a low phase in life or things aren't going well, our first instinct is to try to fix it. Going through a personal loss? *No, we shouldn't feel sad about it, it's a part of life.* Had a rough past? *Oh! Past is past, we should move on.* Someone left? *Oh! It was not meant to be, there are always better people.* Narratives like these are endless and most of the time they don't do any good.

People often tell us, or we tell ourselves, to move on, but it's easier said than done.

For example, birth and death are part of life, but when we experience personal loss, it can leave us feeling shaken and might make us feel that our world has fallen apart. We might experience many negative emotions during this time, so just telling ourselves to move on or not be sad isn't enough.

Think positively?

The most common advice we hear when we complain is to *think positively*. Like it's said, It's good to focus on the positive side of things, but not if it means ignoring the whole situation. As Individuals, we're so focused on thinking positively and moving on that we forget our emotions need time to heal, just like a physical wound.

When we get a scrape, we take care of it, make sure it doesn't get infected, and monitor its healing. But when our emotions are hurt, we often ignore them. We think that by keeping ourselves busy we will be able to feel better, we shove our emotions under the carpet by maintaining a happy face and pretend to be okay without checking in on how we really feel. Over time, as we get busy with new things and our focus shifts, we might think we've moved on from what happened. However, in reality, we never actually dealt with the emotional pain we were experiencing.

A physical wound won't heal properly without proper care, the same goes for emotional pain. Ignoring or suppressing it may seem like avoiding drama, but it actually makes things worse. Emotional pain comes out in uglier ways afterwards if not dealt with properly in the beginning itself.

Emotional Baggage:

Imagine carrying an empty bag and adding heavy stones to it as you go. Without a stop you keep doing it, you think that there's no other way but to carry it all home, because every stone is important. Your shoulders seem to hurt with the weight of the stones, you don't stop adding stones, the bag gets heavier with every step, eventually, the weight becomes too much to move forward. At this point, you have two choices: let go of some stones or stay where you are and not make it home. The same thing goes with memories.

There will be a lot of memories in our lives, good and bad, and there is space both in the conscious and unconscious part of our mind to carry these memories. Painful memories feel heavier, while happy ones are lighter.

With each painful memory we carry, it becomes harder for our mind to handle the emotions that come with it. We face a choice: either letting go of these painful memories or staying stuck with them.

Holding onto them creates emotional baggage, which can affect how we interact with others, how we see things, and how we react to difficult situations, ultimately harming our well-being. But letting go of these painful memories makes room for new memories making us feel lighter.

Many of us believe time heals everything, so we think that the best way to let go of painful memories is to avoid them. This way unknowingly, these memories are sent to the unconscious part of our mind. Just like the conscious part of the mind, our unconscious part bears the weight of these painful memories, which we aren't fully aware of. It subtly changes our personality and makes us behave in ways we never did.

Eventually, unresolved emotions caused by painful memories become too heavy to manage. When this happens, they can surface uncontrollably, leading to unexpected outbursts, stress, or strange behaviours that disrupt our daily life and interactions.

Therefore, it's important to learn healthy ways to move on from negative experiences. This means recognizing our emotions and giving ourselves time to process them.

Letting go and moving on:

Allowing time to process emotions doesn't mean clinging to them for years. Healing is a personal journey, and everyone needs different amounts of time to move on from difficult experiences. However, there is a distinction between actively trying to move forward and simply staying stuck in the same place. Actively moving forward involves engaging in new activities, seeking support, and finding ways to release negative emotions. On the other hand, just letting things remain as they are can lead to stagnation and prevent healing. It's important to find a balance between giving yourself the time you need and taking steps to move past negative feelings.

The three A's of moving on:

The "Three A's of Moving On" are key steps to help you heal from tough experiences and move forward:

Acknowledge: The first step is to recognize your emotions and accept what happened. This means being honest with yourself about the situation and how it has affected you. Acknowledging your feelings is important because it helps you understand what you're going through and starts the healing process.

Accept: Acceptance means coming to terms with what has happened. You don't have to like it, but you need to recognize it as part of your life. Acceptance is about letting go of resisting reality and allowing yourself to feel all your emotions, whether they are anger, sadness, or grief. It's about understanding that some things are beyond your control and it's okay to feel what you feel.

Act: The final step is to take action to heal and move forward. This involves making choices that help you recover and feel better. Actions might include seeking support from friends, family, or professionals, finding new hobbies, setting goals, or practising self-care. By taking these steps, you start to rebuild your life and create positive experiences that help you move on.

Acknowledge	What is the specific event that I want to let go?	
	What are the emotions that I have been feeling?	
Accept	How can I accept this negative event as part of my life without letting it control me?	
Act	Positive steps that I can take..	
	How will letting go make a positive difference in my life?	

Three A's model for moving on

Together, Acknowledge, Accept, and Act provide a solid approach to moving on from difficult situations, supporting emotional healing and personal growth.

CHAPTER IX

Relationships

Relationships are like the ever-changing weather, filled with shifting emotions and experiences. Just as the weather has its seasons, relationships go through ups and downs. There will be windy days when challenges test your bond, storms of conflict and misunderstandings that threaten to push you apart, and rainy moments of tears or doubt that make everything feel heavy.

But there are also gentle breezes—simple, tender moments of care and connection that remind you of the beauty in being together. Light drizzles come as minor disagreements or worries that pass quickly, leaving things clearer and calmer.

And then, there are rainbows—the moments of healing when trust is rebuilt, and love grows stronger. These rainbows are symbols of hope, reminding you of the beauty that follows after facing life's storms together.

Couples who stand by each other through all of life's seasons—the cold winters, heavy rains, and gloomy afternoons—are the ones who build lasting relationships. They hold on with hope, believing that sunny days will return and bright mornings will follow even the darkest nights. By facing each phase with patience, understanding, and care, they create a bond that is resilient and enduring.

Surviving the seasons of change:

Being there for someone in their lowest phase, when they are cranky, unapproachable and moody, might sound romantic and admirable, but it's not easy. Doubts will arise, and you might wonder, *Why am I doing all this? What am I getting in return?* It's natural to feel this way because we all crave love, care, and attention. We want a partner—a safe space to come back to at the end of the day—and we want the love we give to be returned, sometimes even more than we give.

During tough times—when conflicts arise, misunderstandings linger, or emotional distance grows—it can feel like your efforts go unnoticed. You may feel unloved or misunderstood, and even question the value of sharing your thoughts and feelings. The emotional weight can make you hesitate, leaving issues unresolved.

It's easy to hold on to hope: *One day, they'll understand. One day, things will improve. One day, we'll feel close and happy again.* But the truth is, that day won't come if it's only built on silent hope. Subtle hints and waiting for them to notice won't create change.

Change needs action. ***It takes effective communication, addressing and managing hard emotions, and actively working together to rebuild***. Waiting passively will only make the distance grow. To see that brighter day, you must take the first step, no matter how challenging it feels. Relationships don't heal on their own—they heal when both people make an effort to understand, grow, and reconnect.

Effective communication:
Clear and respectful communication is the foundation of any strong relationship. Miscommunication often stems from assumptions, unclear messages, or emotional barriers. Improving your communication skills can transform how you connect with your partner.

Key Tips for Communication:
1. Use "I" Statements
Blaming language can escalate conflicts and create distance

between partners. Instead, frame your feelings and needs using "I" statements. These statements focus on your experience without accusing or attacking the other person.

For example:

- Instead of saying, *"You never listen to me,"* try saying, *"I feel unheard when I don't get a chance to express my thoughts."*
- Instead of saying, *"You're always late,"* try saying, *"I feel frustrated when plans are delayed because I value our time together."*

"I" statements allow you to express your emotions honestly while reducing the likelihood of defensive reactions from your partner. They shift the focus from blame to understanding, creating a safer space for dialogue.

2. Listen Actively

Listening is more than just hearing the words your partner says—it's about truly understanding their perspective. Active listening requires attention, empathy, and a willingness to set aside your own thoughts temporarily.

Steps to practise active listening:

- ***Be Present:*** Put away distractions, like your phone, and give your partner your full attention. This shows that you value what they have to say.
- ***Validate Their Feelings:*** Use phrases like, *"I can see why you'd feel that way,"* or, *"That sounds really difficult."* Validation doesn't mean you agree, but it shows you respect their emotions.
- ***Reflect Back:*** Summarise what your partner has said to ensure you've understood correctly. For instance, *"So you're feeling overwhelmed because of the changes at*

work?" This step helps clarify any misinterpretations.

Active listening builds trust and fosters a deeper connection by making your partner feel heard and understood.

3. Avoid Mind-Reading

One of the most common pitfalls in communication is assuming you know what your partner is thinking or feeling. This habit, often called "mind-reading," can lead to unnecessary misunderstandings and conflict.

For example:

- You might assume your partner is upset because they're quiet, but they may simply be tired.
- You could interpret a delayed text reply as disinterest when it might just be a busy day.

Instead of jumping to conclusions, ask for clarification. Phrases like, *"You seem quiet today—what's on your mind?"* or, *"Is there something bothering you?"* open the door for honest conversation and help avoid miscommunication.

Managing Emotional Reactions:

Relationships often bring out intense emotions. While feelings like love and joy strengthen connections, frustration, anger, and disappointment can strain them. Managing these emotions is essential for maintaining harmony.

Strategies for managing emotional reactions:

1. Pause before reacting

When emotions are intense, the instinct to respond immediately can lead to regrettable words or actions. Instead, take a moment to pause.

How to pause effectively:

- Take a few deep breaths to calm your mind and body.
- Step away from the situation if needed, even for a few minutes, to regain your composure.
- Use this time to ask yourself, *"What do I really want to communicate here?"*

Pausing doesn't mean avoiding the issue—it means approaching it with clarity and intention.

2. Focus on what you can control

In emotionally charged situations, it's easy to fixate on your partner's behaviour, wishing they would act or respond differently. However, the reality is that you can't control their actions, only your own.

Steps to respond calmly:

- Acknowledge your feelings without blaming your partner. For instance, say, "I feel hurt," instead of, *"You made me feel hurt."*
- Approach the conversation with a collaborative mindset, focusing on finding solutions rather than assigning blame.
- When you shift your energy toward what you can control, you create an environment where resolution feels achievable.

3. Label your feelings

Emotions can feel overwhelming when they remain unexamined. Naming your feelings—whether it's anger, sadness, frustration, or disappointment—helps bring clarity to your emotional experience.

How to Label Emotions:

- Pause and reflect on your feelings. Ask yourself, *"What am I truly feeling right now?"*
- Be specific. Instead of saying, *"I'm upset,"* try identifying whether you feel ignored, disrespected, or unappreciated.
- Share your emotions openly with your partner, using "I" statements to express your experience without assigning blame.

For example:

Instead of, *"You never listen to me,"* say, *"I feel unheard when I try to share something important."*

This approach fosters understanding and creates opportunities for meaningful dialogue.

Working together: Building strong and resilient relationships

Healthy relationships aren't about perfection—they're about progress. Mistakes, misunderstandings, and disagreements are inevitable parts of any relationship. What truly matters is how you navigate those challenges, what you learn from them, and how you grow together.

Rather than striving for a flawless relationship, aim for one that evolves with time and effort. Be patient with yourself and your partner. Embrace the idea that both of you will make mistakes, and focus on how you can support each other in learning and improving. Progress, not perfection, is the key to a lasting and fulfilling connection.

Cultivating emotional intimacy

At the heart of every healthy relationship lies emotional intimacy—the deep sense of closeness and connection that comes from knowing and being known by your partner. It's built on trust, vulnerability, and open communication, requiring ongoing effort from both sides.

How to foster emotional intimacy together:

- **Share honestly:** Make space for honest conversations about your thoughts, feelings, and dreams. Sharing openly creates understanding and trust.
- **Be a safe haven:** En11courage your partner to express themselves without fear of judgement. When both partners feel emotionally safe, the bond deepens naturally.
- **Practice empathy:** Even if you don't fully understand your partner's perspective, try to see the situation through their eyes. Empathy helps bridge gaps and strengthens your connection.

Emotional intimacy is not a one-time achievement but a continuous process. By consistently nurturing this connection, you create a foundation of trust and security that can withstand life's inevitable ups and downs.

Creating a vision for your relationship

Every strong relationship thrives on a shared vision—a clear understanding of what you want to build together. This vision gives your partnership purpose and direction, acting as a compass when challenges arise.

Steps to create a shared vision:

- **Reflect on values:** Take time to discuss what matters most to each of you. What do you value in life, and how do those values align with your relationship?
- **Set goals together:** Talk about the life you want to create as a team. Consider everything from personal goals to shared dreams.
- **Stay aligned:** Regularly revisit your shared vision to ensure you're both on the same path and working

toward the same goals.

Asking reflective questions like *"What kind of life do we want to create?"* or *"How can we support each other's dreams?"* fosters a sense of alignment. Even during difficult times, having a shared vision keeps you motivated and reminds you of the bigger picture you're working toward.

Handling challenges as a team

No relationship is immune to challenges. Whether it's a minor disagreement or a major life hurdle, the way you handle these moments can either strengthen or weaken your bond. The key lies in facing them as a team, rather than as individuals on opposing sides.

Working through difficulties together:

- **Seek solutions, not victory:** Approach conflicts with a collaborative mindset. Focus on resolving the issue rather than proving who's right.
- **Reassure each other:** During tough times, remind your partner that you're in this together. A simple acknowledgment like *"We'll figure this out"* can provide comfort and reassurance.

When challenges arise, remember that they're opportunities for growth. By tackling them side by side, you reinforce your connection and build trust in your ability to navigate life together.

Looking forward, together

In the end, building a lasting relationship isn't about avoiding hardships or seeking constant happiness. It's about finding joy in the journey, supporting each other through the storms, and holding on tightly even when the winds threaten to pull you apart. It's about standing together in the face of challenges and finding moments of light and hope, even in the darkest times.

CHAPTER X

Finding happiness

Happiness is a universal desire. It's not just an emotion but a state of being that brings a sense of fulfilment, peace, and purpose to life. Yet, in the complexities of everyday existence, happiness can feel elusive, slipping through your fingers just when you think you've found it.

But what if happiness wasn't something you had to chase? What if it was already within you, waiting to be nurtured? Finding happiness isn't about fixing your life or reaching a perfect moment; it's about creating conditions where joy, meaning, and contentment can thrive. This chapter will guide you on a journey to uncover what makes life truly worthwhile and how you can cultivate lasting happiness in your day-to-day experience.

Redefining happiness

Happiness is often misunderstood. It's easy to associate it with fleeting pleasures, success, or possessions, but these provide only temporary satisfaction. True happiness runs deeper; it's a sense of alignment between your values, actions, and aspirations.

At its core, happiness is about feeling connected—to yourself, to others, and to a purpose that gives your life meaning. It's about recognizing what truly matters and investing your energy in ways that bring a sense of fulfilment.

To begin this journey, take a moment to reflect: What does happiness mean to you? By clarifying your vision of happiness, you create a foundation for cultivating it in your life.

Discovering your inner compass

Happiness is deeply personal, and its path is unique for each individual. While external factors like relationships, health, and circumstances can influence your happiness, the true source lies within you.

Start by exploring what brings you a sense of joy and purpose. These moments may seem small—a conversation that leaves you smiling, a task that engages your full attention, or a quiet moment of gratitude. These experiences provide clues about what fulfils you.

Your inner compass is shaped by your values, passions, and strengths. When your actions align with these elements, happiness follows naturally. By tuning into this compass, you can navigate life with greater clarity and intention.

The power of gratitude

Gratitude is a cornerstone of happiness. When you take the time to appreciate what you have, rather than focusing on what's missing, you shift your perspective. Gratitude helps you see life's abundance, even in challenging times, and creates space for joy to flourish.

Make it a habit to notice the small moments of beauty and kindness around you. It could be the warmth of the sun, the sound of laughter, or a gesture of support from someone you care about. These moments may seem ordinary, but they're the building blocks of a happy life.

As you practise gratitude, you'll find that it opens the door to more positive experiences. It's not about ignoring life's difficulties; it's about balancing them with a deep appreciation for what's good.

Cultivating connections

Happiness thrives in connection. Relationships, whether with family, friends, or your community, provide a sense of belonging and support that enriches your life.

Take the time to nurture these connections. Listen with presence, express your appreciation, and share your moments of joy. These simple acts strengthen the bonds that sustain you.

Connection isn't just about others; it's also about your relationship with yourself. Treat yourself with kindness and compassion, recognizing that your happiness is just as important as anyone else's.

Embracing growth

Happiness isn't about staying in a bubble of comfort. It's about embracing growth and challenging yourself in ways that expand your potential. When you pursue activities that stretch your skills, spark your curiosity, or align with your passions, you experience a sense of progress and achievement that contributes to happiness.

This growth doesn't have to be monumental. It can be as simple as learning something new, taking on a creative project, or stepping outside your routine. These experiences add richness to your life and remind you of your capacity to evolve.

Creating balance

Happiness flourishes in balance. It's about finding harmony between the different aspects of your life—work, relationships, health, and personal interests. When one area demands too much of your energy, it can leave you feeling depleted.

Take time to reflect on how you're spending your energy. Are there areas that need more attention? Are there ways to simplify or delegate tasks that feel overwhelming?

Creating balance is an ongoing process. It requires you to listen to your needs, set boundaries, and make choices that honour your well-being. When you prioritise balance, you create space for happiness to take root.

Living with intention

Happiness often comes from living with intention—being mindful of your choices and aligning them with what truly matters to you. This doesn't mean every moment has to be profound; it means approaching life with a sense of purpose and presence.

Ask yourself: What kind of life do I want to create? How do I want to spend my time and energy? By answering these questions, you can begin to shape your days in a way that feels meaningful and fulfilling.

Living with intention also means letting go of what doesn't serve you. This might include habits, thoughts, or commitments that drain your energy without adding value to your life.

Embracing joy in the everyday

Happiness isn't found in grand gestures or extraordinary moments alone—it's woven into the fabric of everyday life. It's in the small rituals that bring comfort, the moments of laughter, and the simple acts of kindness.

Pay attention to these moments. Savour your morning coffee, enjoy the rhythm of a favourite song, or take a moment to appreciate a beautiful sunset. By noticing and cherishing these small joys, you cultivate a sense of happiness that endures.

Moving forward

Happiness is not a destination; it's a journey. It's about creating a life that feels rich and meaningful, one step at a time.

You have the ability to shape your experience, to create moments of joy and purpose, and to live a life that reflects your values. With each small step, you move closer to the happiness you seek—not as something outside of you, but as a reflection of the life you're building within.

Happiness is yours to cultivate, yours to embrace, and yours to share with the world. Let it begin here, in this moment, with the choices you make and the life you create.

CHAPTER XI

Making a change

Change can feel overwhelming because it often means leaving your comfort zone and stepping into the unknown. Even habits that no longer serve you can feel safer than the uncertainty of trying something new. This fear is natural, but it shouldn't stop you.

Wanting to change is a sign of growth. It shows you've realized something in your life could improve—whether it's your mindset, habits, relationships, or goals. This awareness reflects hope and a belief that life can be better.

The journey to change isn't always easy. There will be doubts, challenges, and setbacks. However, every small step forward builds your confidence and helps you grow. Over time, the discomfort fades, and the new becomes familiar—a life that better reflects your values and goals.

Understanding the desire to change

Change often stems from a need to close the gap between where you are and where you want to be. It could be about improving your health, finding greater happiness, or building better relationships. The first step towards change is by identifying what drives your desire.

Spend some time reflecting on why this change matters to you. Ask yourself questions like:

- What would my life look like if I achieved this change?
- How would I feel about myself?
- What benefits would this bring to those I care about?

By connecting deeply with your reasons for change, you build a foundation of motivation that will support you when challenges arise.

Defining your goals

Clarity is key when it comes to making a change. A vague desire to *"do better"* or *"improve"* is not enough to guide you. Instead, create a clear vision of what you want to achieve.

- **Be specific:** Define your goals in detail. For instance, instead of saying, *"I want to be healthier,"* state, *"I want to eat balanced meals and exercise three times a week."*
- **Be realistic:** Start with goals that are achievable within your current circumstances. Overambitious goals can lead to frustration and discouragement.
- **Set a timeline:** Establish a timeframe for your goals, even if it's flexible. Having a sense of when you want to see progress keeps you focused.

Your goals should be meaningful to you. They should align with your values and reflect what truly matters in your life.

Identifying obstacles

The journey of change is rarely smooth, once you Identify what change you want to make and start working on your goals, setbacks are going to be a natural part of the process. As you commit to your goals, challenges will inevitably arise. External obstacles—like time constraints, lack of resources, or limited support—can slow your progress, while Internal obstacles rooted in your thoughts, beliefs, and emotions can manifest as self-doubt, fear of failure, or resistance to stepping outside your comfort zone. These barriers are not signs of weakness but reflections of the mind's natural tendency to seek safety and avoid risk.

Understanding this can help you approach setbacks with compassion rather than frustration.

Remember, setbacks are not the end of the road—they're part of the learning process. Each challenge provides valuable insight, revealing what works, what doesn't, and where adjustments are needed.

Dealing with setbacks

Instead of seeing setbacks as failures, view them as opportunities to learn and adjust.

When a setback occurs:

Pause and reflect: Take a moment to pause and reflect on the situation. Avoid reacting impulsively or judging yourself harshly. Instead, ask yourself:

- What led to this setback?
- Was it due to a lack of preparation, unforeseen external stressors, or overestimating what I could handle?
- Are there patterns or triggers I can identify that contributed to this moment?

Reflection is key to understanding the root causes of a setback and prevents repeating the same mistakes.

Reframe the experience: The language you use to describe a setback matters. Instead of saying, *"I failed,"* adopt a growth-oriented mindset and say, *"I'm learning"* or *"I'll try a different approach."* This simple shift helps you focus on possibilities and solutions rather than dwelling on negative emotions.

Adjust your strategy: Use the insights gained from reflection to adjust your plan. If you struggled with time management, consider scheduling your tasks differently. If emotional overwhelm played a role, find ways to address your stress before tackling your goals.

Breaking down the process:
Big changes can feel overwhelming, especially when you think about all the steps required. The key is to break the process into smaller, manageable pieces. Each small step you take builds momentum and makes the larger goal feel achievable.

Build momentum: Every small step creates momentum, and momentum is powerful. Think of it as a snowball effect: the more you accomplish, the more energy and confidence you gain to tackle the next step. Even on days when progress feels slow, remember that every step forward, no matter how small, brings you closer to your goal.

Focus on the present: Avoid getting lost in the enormity of your goal. Concentrate on what you can do today. Change happens in small, consistent actions rather than dramatic leaps.

Celebrate progress: Acknowledge even the smallest victories. Each step forward is a reminder of your capability and commitment to change.

Stay connected to your why: As you take small, purposeful steps, keep your ultimate goal in focus. Remind yourself why this change is important and how it aligns with what truly matters to you. Your "why" acts as a guide, giving meaning to your efforts and keeping you motivated.

Developing new habits:
Change is sustained through habits. The behaviors and patterns you repeat daily form the foundation of your life. To make a change stick, focus on creating habits that support your goals.

Start small: Trying to overhaul your life overnight is a recipe for burnout. Instead, introduce small changes that are easy to maintain. For instance, if you want to improve your mental health, start by dedicating five minutes a day to mindfulness or journaling.

Be consistent: Habits take time to form. Consistency is more important than intensity. Show up for yourself every day, even if it's in small ways.

Build a support system: Surround yourself with people who encourage and support your efforts. Share your goals with trusted friends or family members, and don't hesitate to seek help when needed.

Track your progress: Monitoring your habits can be a powerful motivator. Keep a journal, use an app, or simply mark your calendar to track your daily efforts. Seeing your progress visually can boost your confidence and reinforce your commitment to change.

Be patient with yourself: Habits take time to develop. It's natural to encounter setbacks or moments when motivation wanes. Be kind to yourself during these times and remember why you started. Reflect on how even small, consistent changes are bringing you closer to your larger goal.

Sustaining long-term change:
Change isn't just about reaching a goal; it's about creating a lasting transformation. To sustain your progress:

Make it part of your routine: Integrate new behaviors into your daily life until they become habits.

Stay flexible: Be willing to adjust your approach as your circumstances and priorities evolve.

Reflect regularly: Periodically review your goals and progress to ensure they still align with your values and aspirations.

Cultivate a growth mindset: Sustaining long-term change requires embracing a mindset of growth and learning. Recognize that setbacks and challenges are natural parts of the process. Instead of viewing them as failures, see them as opportunities to learn and grow.

Coming to the end:

As you near the end of this book, you might feel that some strategies will work for you while others may not. This is perfectly normal. However, it's important to remember that change begins with action. Simply thinking that something is helpful or promising is not enough. If you don't take action, it won't lead to any real change.

You don't need to apply everything you've read all at once. Instead, focus on incorporating one thing at a time as you navigate different challenges in your life. The key to success lies in your belief that what you're trying can work for you, and how consistently you put in the effort each day. Change takes time and dedication, so take it one step at a time and be patient with yourself as you move forward.

About The Author

Sharad Raj C is a psychologist, author, and founder of *Scribbled Thoughts*, an online platform for writers with over 130,000 followers on Instagram. With extensive experience in counseling, he has conducted more than five hundred counselling sessions, guiding people through mental health challenges and personal growth.

Sharad also runs Therapy with Sharad, a dedicated platform where he provides therapy sessions tailored to individual needs. He primarily works with individuals aged 15–25, addressing issues such as stress, anxiety, peer pressure, interpersonal conflicts, lack of motivation, performance anxiety, self-doubt, and grief.

His empathetic and relatable approach has made him a trusted counselor for young people navigating the complexities of adolescence and early adulthood. In addition, Sharad has experience working with clients from diverse age groups, offering them support in overcoming life's challenges and finding clarity.

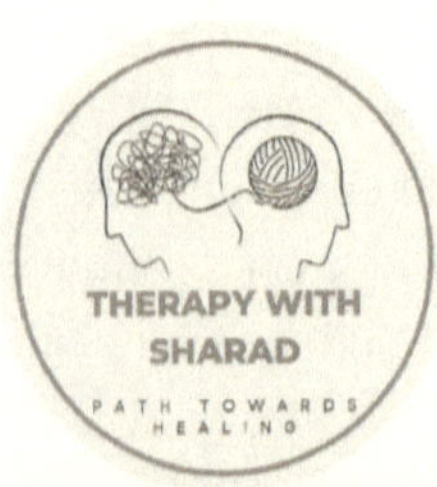

THERAPY WITH SHARAD!

Therapy with sharad is an online counseling platform started by Sharad Raj C, it is still in the developing phase, but the plan is to make mental health services accessible to everyone with a budget friendly approach.

To book a counselling session at Therapy with sharad, drop an email on Therapywithsharad@gmail.com

BRING SHARAD RAJ C TO YOUR ORGANIZATION!

Sharad Raj C is a psychologist with an experience of conducting different workshops related to emotional well-being of Individuals. He also has experience with conducting group sessions and seminars to address different mental health challenges.

To bring Sharad Raj C to your organization, drop an email on sharadrajc97@gmail.com

ALSO A FICTIONAL WRITER!

Check out other books by Sharad Raj C on Amazon